ROMAN TRADE AND TRAVEL

PETER HODGE
Principal teacher of Classics
Lenzie Academy

LONGMAN

1 : TRAVELLERS' TRAILS

From the earliest times men have travelled. But why do people travel?

The photographs here show some examples of different types of modern transport and the people who use them. Can you tell what kind of people are shown and why they are travelling?

A horse-drawn cart with passengers

What sort of people travelled in Roman times? And why did they travel?

To find the answers to these questions, we must look at various kinds of evidence and follow the trails left by Roman travellers, just as we might track down someone from his footprints and other clues he has dropped.

One problem is that just following a person's tracks does not always tell us what sort of person made them, but we can sometimes use clues to make sensible guesses. For example, look at the two photographs here. What clues do they give us about the kind of travellers they are, how they are travelling and why?

A boat being towed along a canal. What cargo is being carried?

Paintings, mosaics, pictures and inscriptions carved on tombstones and monuments can sometimes give us useful clues about Roman travellers, including their names, what they did and why they travelled, and where they came from.

Some Romans wrote letters. From these we can also get clues about the writers.

In the following extract from a letter to a friend the famous Roman politician Cicero is describing part of a journey he made from Rome to Asia Minor (modern Turkey) in 51 BC.

At present I am finishing the journey to my province of Cilicia (where Cicero was going as Governor) on a hot and dusty road. . . . I hope to arrive on the first of August.

CICERO *Letters to Atticus* V 14 1

Roman soldiers on the march, crossing a pontoon bridge (a bridge made of boats)

Letters provide us with information about travellers and also about Roman postal services, as you can see from the two letters.

A letter from Egypt

From: Rustus Barbarus
To: his brother Pompeius

Greetings. How come you haven't answered my letter if you received the loaves of bread? I sent you 15 loaves with Popillius and Dutuporis, and another 15 and a vase with Draco the carter.... I also sent you 6 with Thiadices, the army cavalryman, who said he could take them with him.... By the way, I'm getting married. As soon as I am, I'll write you to come. Cheerio.

A letter from a Roman Governor to the Emperor

From: Pliny, Governor of Bithynia (in Turkey)
To: Emperor Trajan

Your Highness, until now I have not granted a permit to use the Imperial Postal Service to anyone except for official business. But I've had to break the rule because of an emergency. My wife heard that her grandfather had died and wanted to hurry to be by her aunt.... I felt sure you would approve when you heard of the personal reason for the journey.

PLINY *Letters* X 120

Compare the modern Post Office van (*above*) with a carriage of the Roman Imperial Postal Service (*below*). What are the differences?

The Romans travelled by river and sea as well as by land. Some of this evidence, like the picture here and the account (right), also tells us about the kind of people who were travelling and why they were travelling.

When it was decided that we were to sail for Italy, Paul and the other prisoners went on board a ship bound for Turkey under the supervision of an army officer named Julius. . . . When they reached Myra, the officer found a grain ship from Alexandria (in Egypt) bound for Italy and put us on board.
Acts of the Apostles 27 1

What clues do the painting and the account give us about these Roman travellers and the reasons for their journeys?

A ship called the Isis Giminiana being loaded with grain. The name of the ship's owner is Farnaces.

QUESTIONS

1 How can we tell what kinds of people travelled in Roman times? Write down the main kinds of evidence we have. (pages 3–6)

2 Why were the men in the photographs on page 3 travelling? How can we tell?

3 What are the men doing in the photograph on page 4? How are they travelling and why?

4 Why was Cicero travelling to Turkey? How do we know? (page 4)

5 Write down two ways in which Rustus Barbarus had sent parcels to his brother. (page 5)

6 What kind of person used the Imperial Postal Service? (page 5) Why had Pliny's wife been travelling?

7 What kind of person would have travelled in the carriage in the photograph on page 5? What clues suggest this?

8 What kind of man was Farnaces, who is shown in the photograph on page 6? What clues does the painting give us?

9 Why were Paul and the others travelling to Rome? (page 6) How were they travelling and how do we know?

THINGS TO DO

1 Make a list of the various reasons why people travel nowadays and the kinds of travellers. Then make a list of the various Roman travellers you have met in this chapter. Add to your list as you come across new examples.

2 Look at one of the pictures of Roman travellers in this chapter. Imagine that you are the person in the picture. Make up a story or a letter to a friend describing a journey. Include such things as who you are, why you are making the trip, how you travel, and the problems you have.

2: ALL ROADS LEAD TO ROME

Trade routes

Long before there were proper roads people travelled from one place to another in search of food or pastures for their animals, and to trade with the inhabitants of other villages and settlements. The early tracks trodden by men and animals gradually became used by traders to carry their goods from one settlement to the next. These trading routes wound across the countryside of Italy, through the valleys and over the hills. Whenever the route came to a river, there was a ferry, or else the track wound up river until there was a fording place where the river was shallow enough for men and animals to cross on foot.

An example of an early trade route is the *Via Salaria*, or 'Salt Road', which was used by traders to carry salt from the mountains to the north-east of Rome down river to Rome itself. (This was because the Samnites, an Italian tribe living to the south, would not allow the Romans to take salt from the sea.)

The following passage describes a similar kind of overland trade route used by traders carrying tin from Britain to Marseilles at the mouth of the River Rhône in the south of France.

The traders who buy tin in Britain transport it over to Gaul (modern France), which they cross on foot in 30 days, using pack horses to carry it, until they reach the mouth of the River Rhône.

DIODORUS SICULUS V 22

The Via Appia (just outside Rome), which is still used today for herding sheep and for ordinary traffic

Main roads

As Rome began to conquer the neighbouring tribes and to expand her power throughout the whole of Italy, people began to realise that proper roads were needed for transporting troops and supplies from one part of the country to another.

The first recorded road in Italy that we know about was built in 312 BC when Appius Claudius was **censor** (the man responsible for public works).

That year (312 BC) was marked by the censorship of Appius Claudius . . . who is remembered because he built a road.
LIVY *The History of Rome* IX 29

The *Via Appia* (or 'Appius' Road') was originally built from Rome to Capua, a distance of 132 miles (211 kilometres), and followed the route of the old dirt track. It was the first of the many main roads that were built in Italy during the next two hundred years.

These main roads were usually named after the man who organised the building of them. Later they were named after the emperor in whose reign they were built.

Part of the Via Appia where the original stones can still be seen. It is still used today.

Main Roman roads in Italy

The map and the table show how the main Roman roads in
Italy gradually were built until they formed a network across
the whole country.

Road	Route	Date
Via Appia	Rome to Capua	312 BC
Via Aurelia	Rome to Pisa	241 BC
	(extended by Via Aemilia Scauri 109 BC)	
Via Flaminia	Rome to Ariminum	220 BC
	(extended to Brundisium 148–132 BC)	
Via Aemilia	Ariminum to Placentia	187 BC
Via Cassia	Rome to Arretium	177 BC
	(extended to Pisa 140–125 BC)	
Via Postumia	Genoa to Cremona	
Via Egnatia	built from Jugoslavia to Greece	145 BC
Via Popilia	Capua to Rhegium	132 BC
Via Ostiensis	Rome to Ostia rebuilt by Claudius	40 AD
Via Domitiana	Sinuessa to Naples	80 AD
Via Traiana	(extended Via Appia from Beneventum to Brundisium)	114 AD

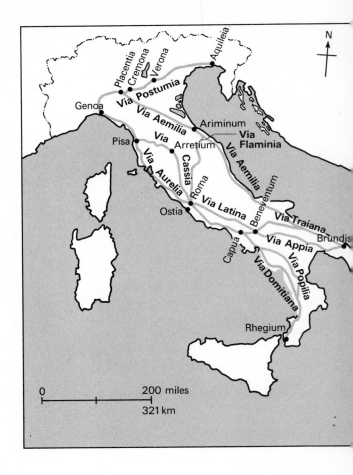

Types of roads

What were Roman roads like? And how do we know?

Most of our knowledge comes from parts of Roman roads that are now modern roads, and from remains which have been uncovered by archaeologists. From these we can see that there were several different kinds of roads.

Some were just dirt tracks or country roads (called *Viae Terrenae*) made of earth or grit, which became very muddy when it rained. They were little more than old tracks or drove roads.

In other parts of the country where material for road building was available, the Romans built gravel roads (called *Viae Glareae*). These were second-class roads which could take heavier traffic.

Main roads like the Via Appia and Via Flaminia were first-class roads made of interlocking stone slabs (called *Viae Stratae*). These were so well built that many of them are still in use today, as you can see in the photograph here.

Part of the Via Flaminia today, showing the paved Roman road with the modern tarmac road beside it

Road building methods

Before a new road was built, army surveyors and engineers surveyed the route and cleared the ground.

Roman surveyors used an instrument called a **groma** for working out the line of a road. The surveyor (called an **agrimensor** = land measurer) planted the upright pole in the ground. At the top of this were two wooden arms on a pivot and at right angles to each other. From each arm hung a line with a lead weight (the modern 'plumb-line', which comes from the Latin word **plumbum** = lead). A man with a pole went on ahead a short distance. The surveyor then looked along one of the cross-arms of the **groma** and shouted instructions to the man with the pole until it was lined up in a straight line with the part of the road that had already been built. Then a trench was dug to mark the line of the new stretch of road.

Students with a *groma* (used for working out the line of a road), which they have made on the model of a Roman one. On the right is a modern theodolite used for the same purpose by surveyors now.

Roman roads ran straight wherever possible; a straight line is the shortest distance between two points, and Roman roads were originally built to transport soldiers and supplies as fast as possible from one part of the country to another. Many modern roads, in Britain, like those shown on page 19, follow the line of Roman roads, because the Roman surveyors made such a fine job of siting their roads.

The Roman writer Statius (who lived from 40–96 AD) describes how a first-class road was built to Naples. The following description was written to mark the opening of the Via Domitiana by the Emperor Domitian in 80 AD.

First there's the job of marking a furrow, opening up a track and excavating a trench.

Next the trench must be refilled with material packed down as a foundation for the surface of the road; the ground must not give way when the stone slabs are laid.

When they've been laid, they are held in place by kerb stones and lots of wedges.

Look at all the gangs of men at work!

Some are busy felling trees and clearing hillsides; others are cutting and smoothing rocks and planing enormous wooden beams, while stonemasons cement the stones together with lime and tufa (volcanic ash used for cement). Others work hard to divert the course of streams and pump out the water that fills the trenches. The countryside and waving woods all round are filled with noise and the sound of workmen.

STATIUS *Poems* IV 3

Compare Statius' description with the diagrams on the next page showing the stages in the building of a Roman road.

Cross-section of a Roman first-class road

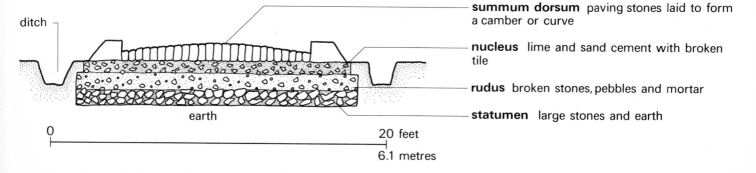

ditch

summum dorsum paving stones laid to form a camber or curve

nucleus lime and sand cement with broken tile

rudus broken stones, pebbles and mortar

statumen large stones and earth

earth

0   20 feet

6.1 metres

14

Stages in the building of a Roman road

Stage 1: Surveying the line of the road

Stage 2: Excavating a trench and laying the foundations

Stage 3: Building up the layers

Stage 4: Laying the paved surface and kerbing

Milestones

In 123 BC the tribune Caius Gracchus organised the putting up of stone pillars at intervals along the main roads leading from Rome. These 'milestones' (called **miliaria** from the Latin **mille passus** = 1000 paces or 1 Roman mile; 1 Roman mile = 1611 yards or 1481.5 metres) are often inscribed with the name of an emperor or the person who built or repaired the road. They show the distance between where they stand and the nearest town, or the distance from them to the Golden Milestone which stood in the centre of Rome.

The photograph here shows one of the milestones on the Via Appia-Traiana between Beneventum and Brundisium.

The inscription reads as follows:

V
IMP·CAESAR·
DIVI·NERVAE·F·
NERVA·TRAIANVS·
AVG·GERM·DACIC·
PONT·MAX·TR·POT·
XIII·IMP·VI·COS·V·
P·P
VIAM·A·BENEVENTO
BRVNDISIVM·PECVN·
SVA·FECIT

And here is a translation:

MILESTONE V
EMPEROR CAESAR,
SON OF GOD-LIKE NERVA,
NERVA TRAIANUS (i.e. TRAJAN)
AUGUSTUS, CONQUEROR OF GERMANY & DACIA
CHIEF PRIEST, TRIBUNE'S POWER FOR THE
XIIITH TIME, EMPEROR FOR THE VITH TIME
CONSUL FOR THE VTH TIME
FATHER OF HIS COUNTRY,
THE ROAD FROM BENEVENTUM ·
TO BRUNDISIUM WITH HIS OWN MONEY
MADE

Note: Trajan became Emperor—**imperator**—in 98 AD. He was acclaimed *imperator* 'for the VIth time' in 106 AD.

Tunnels, bridges and aqueducts

There were occasions when the Roman surveyors were faced with obstacles which forced them either to alter the line of the road or to try to overcome them in some way. Just how successful Roman engineers were at overcoming obstacles can still be seen to this day.

When part of the Via Flaminia was extended northwards through the mountains, the Romans dug a tunnel through the rock at a place called the Furlo Pass. Above the north-east entrance to the tunnel is the following inscription:

EMPEROR CAESAR AUGUSTUS VESPASIANUS
CHIEF PRIEST, VIITH TIME AS TRIBUNE,
VITH TIME AS EMPEROR, FATHER OF HIS COUNTRY,
VIIITH TIME AS CONSUL, CENSOR
SAW TO THE BUILDING OF THIS

Vespasian became Emperor in 69 AD.

The Via Flaminia tunnel at the Furlo Pass

But perhaps the most spectacular examples of the skill with which Roman engineers overcame obstacles are to be seen in the bridges and aqueducts (used for carrying water to towns) they built in different parts of the Empire. At Alcantara in Spain a Roman bridge spans the River Tagus. It was built by Gaius Julius Lacer in 105 AD and is 600 feet long and 150 feet high at its central point. On the centre arch are inscribed the words:

PONTEM PERFECI MANSURUM IN SAECULA

meaning:

I HAVE BUILT A BRIDGE THAT WILL LAST FOR AGES

You can see from the photograph how right he was.

The Roman bridge at Alcantara in Spain

Expansion of the road system

Throughout the first century AD the Romans expanded their road system as Roman armies conquered new territories. By the end of the first century most of Britain, Gaul (modern France), Germany and Spain was covered by a network of roads that had been built by Roman engineers with the help of slaves and the inhabitants of the countries through which they ran.

The map here shows the main Roman roads in Britain. Of these the most important were:

Name of road	Route
Watling Street	Dover – London – Chester
Ermine Street	London – Lincoln – York
Stane Street	London – Chichester
Port Way – Ackling Dyke	London – Silchester – Old Sarum – Dorchester
Fosse Way	Exeter – Bath – Cirencester – Leicester – Lincoln
Ryknield Way	Bourton-on-the-Water – Derby – Chesterfield
Icknield Way	St. Albans – Great Chesterford
Akeman Street	Cirencester – St. Albans – Cambridge
Great Road	London – Colchester
Dere Street	York – Corbridge – Melrose

Main Roman roads and towns in Britain

The photographs show examples of Roman roads in Britain—as you can see them today.

The Cirencester-Winchester road

Watling Street in Kent (with the modern M2 on the right)

Network of Roman roads throughout the Empire in 120 AD

A network spanning an empire

By about 120 AD the Romans had built up a network of roads that linked the forty-three provinces of the Empire and covered over 50,000 miles. The main routes of this network radiated out from Rome, the capital of the Empire. It is hardly surprising that people said: 'All roads lead to Rome.'

QUESTIONS

1 What kind of roads were the Via Salaria and other early roads? (page 8)

2 What was the name of the first recorded proper Roman road that we know about? When was it built? How did it get its name? (page 9)

3 Write down three main types of Roman roads. How do we know about them? (page 11)

4 Look at Statius' description of how a road was built (page 13).
   a) Write down the stages in its building that he mentions.
   b) What kind of a road is he describing?
   c) What did the Romans use for cementing the stones together?
   d) What other jobs were going on while the road was being laid?

5 Look at the inscription on page 15. Trajan became Emperor in 98 AD. In what year was the road from Beneventum to Brundisium opened? How can we tell?

6 Name two examples of the way in which Roman road-builders overcame obstacles. How can we tell they were built by the Romans? (pages 16–17)

7 Look at the map of roads in Britain on page 18 and find the names of the roads that take the following routes:
   a) London to Chester
   b) London to Dorchester
   c) London to York
   d) London to Chichester
   e) Exeter to Lincoln
   f) London to Colchester
   g) York to Melrose

8 Look at the photographs on page 19. What feature of the way Roman roads were built is shown?

THINGS TO DO

1 Draw a large-scale map of the main Roman roads in Britain from the Ordnance Survey map, marking in the names of the roads and the main towns and cities through which they ran.

2 Look at the pictures on page 14. Make a wall-chart comparing the way a Roman road was built with the stages in the building of a modern motorway. Number each stage and write a short description of each.

3 Compare Roman milestones with modern road signs. What kind of information does each give? In what ways are they different? (page 15)

4 Using a modern map or road atlas of Europe and the map on page 20:
   a) Write down the modern names of the countries linked by the Roman road network.
   b) Which modern motorways follow the same routes as part of the Roman road systems?

3: ROAD TRAVEL

A journey by road from Rome to Brundisium

Travel even on good roads was a slow business. In 38 BC the poet Horace travelled by road from Rome to Brundisium (modern Brindisi on the coast of the Adriatic Sea), a distance of 366 miles (576 kilometres). Below is an outline of the journey based on his description.

	Stage of journey	Distance (miles)
Day 1:	Rome to Aricia	15 miles
Day 2:	Aricia to Forum Appii	23 miles
Day 3:	Canal boat to Feronia	15 miles
	Feronia to Anxur	4 miles
	Anxur to Fundi	13 miles
	Fundi to Formiae	15 miles
Day 4:	Formiae to Sinuessa	24 miles
Day 5:	Sinuessa to Capua	35 miles
	Capua to Caudium	20 miles
Day 6:	Caudium to Beneventum	15 miles
Day 7:	Beneventum to Trivicum	23 miles
Day 8:	By coach to Ausculum	28 miles
Day 9:	Ausculum to Canusium	30 miles
	Canusium to Rubi	25 miles
Day 10:	Rubi to Barium (on a bad road)	23 miles
Day 11:	Barium to Gnathia (later Egnatia)	30 miles
Day 12:	Gnathia to Brundisium	38 miles

When Horace travelled this route there was no first-class road beyond Beneventum. Find the places Horace passed through on the map.

Kinds of transport

How you travelled depended on who you were and the kind of road you were travelling on.

The poor walked or rode on mules. Mules were used on bad roads in hilly country and for towing boats along canals like the one on which Horace travelled to cross the marshes between Forum Appii and Feronia.

Farmers and peasants used carts drawn by mules or horses to carry goods to market in the nearby towns.

Horace probably covered the first part of his journey in a slow-moving carriage or on a mule. The luggage was carried in packs slung on either side of the mules.

A farmer with his cart drawn by two horses. The cart is loaded with an ox-hide of wine (casks were not yet in common use).

Coaches

The rich could afford to travel in more comfort by coach. The Romans used two main kinds—a four-wheeled carriage (called a **raeda**), and two-wheeled vehicles like the **cisium** and the **carpentum**.

The *raeda* was slow; its average speed was probably not more than three or four miles per hour. On good roads the fastest form of travel was horse or two-wheeled gig.

Reconstruction of a four-wheeled carriage (*raeda*)

For longer journeys on first-class roads you could travel by a sleeping coach, which was fitted with curtains and cushions. This was used by the wealthy and by government officials travelling to and from the different provinces of the empire.

A two-wheeled vehicle (*carpentum*) shown on a Roman coin (enlarged)

Problems of road travel

Travel was often uncomfortable and sometimes dangerous as you can see from the following description:

In the old days the traveller in his slow carriage
Swung from side to side and held on tight
With only a pair of wheels to save him from the marsh
That swallowed them up to their axles.
Latins knew all about being shipwrecked all right. . . .
But on dry land!
STATIUS *Poems* IV 3

The writer Seneca describes an uncomfortable journey from Baiae on the coast to Naples.

The road was so deep in mud we might as well have gone by sea. . . . And then after being splattered with mud we were dusted with sand in the Naples tunnel. The torches in that suffocating tunnel only made you more aware how dark it was and dusty.
SENECA *Moral Letters* 57

Travellers were sometimes set upon by robbers.

At one time Italy was controlled by tribes who were poor and used to rob folk. But now they have either been wiped out or so completely conquered that you can trust them, and the roads, thanks to the engineers, are passable. It was Augustus who finally put down bandits by building roads.
STRABO *Geography* IV 6 6

A four-wheeled covered coach used in the Imperial Post

The Imperial Post

As the Romans built up a network of first-class roads linking the provinces, an official express service was introduced for carrying official letters and messengers. This was the Imperial Post (called the **Cursus Publicus** or 'official travel'). The writer Suetonius says that the Emperor Augustus started it.

To enable reports of what was happening in all the provinces to be carried faster, Augustus placed young men first of all and later coaches at short intervals along the military roads. The idea of coaches was better because the same man could bring a message and be questioned about it.
SUETONIUS *Life of Augustus* 49 3

Each official courier was given a permit (called a **diploma**) issued by the government, and only a person with this permit could use the service. (Look back at the letter written by Pliny to the Emperor Trajan which appears on page 5.)

Staging-posts, inns and hospitality

The official courier stopped at a government staging-post at regular intervals along the journey in order to change the horses, have a meal or spend the night before travelling on. These staging-posts (called **stationes**, from which we get our word 'station') were spaced out at intervals of about 20–25 miles (32–40 kilometres) and a good messenger would usually cover five stages in a single day, we are told.

The ordinary traveller, however, broke his journey and spent the night either at an inn (**taberna**) or at a friend's house. Roman inns had a bad reputation. Writers like Horace complain that they were dirty, the beds infested with bugs, and the inn-keepers were scoundrels who charged high prices for poor service. Brawls were frequent and travellers were often robbed while they slept, or even murdered. Because of this many Romans tried to spend the night with friends, where they could enjoy a comfortable bed and friendly hospitality as well as exchanging the latest news or telling stories.

Inn-keeper, let's settle up.
One bottle of wine, and one
loaf of bread   — 1 as.
Some stew   — 2 asses;
agreed. The girl — 8 asses;
that's right. Fodder for
the mule   — 2 asses.

Found in an inn in Aesernia.
An *as* was a bronze or copper Roman coin.
4 asses = 1 sestertius.

VIBIUS SLEPT HERE ALONE
LONGING FOR HIS GIRL
URBANA

Scrawled on a wall in Pompeii

ACCOMMODATION TO LET

ROOM WITH THREE BEDS
AND ALL CONVENIENCES

An advertisement from Pompeii

Distances and speed of travel

How fast you could travel along Roman roads depended on the kind of country, the type of road and the way you were travelling.

Look back at the outline of Horace's journey you saw on page 22 and then compare it with the following account. For example, where the people mentioned were travelling, how they were travelling, how far, and how long their journeys took them. Then try to work out the average distance covered each day by doing the following calculation:

$$\text{Average mileage per day} = \frac{\text{Total distance travelled (in miles)}}{\text{Total number of days taken}}$$

A journey from Rome to Germany

The Emperor Tiberius completed the longest twenty-four hours journey by coach ever recorded when hurrying to his brother Drusus who was ill in Germany. He covered 200 (Roman) miles (= 183 modern miles) in 24 hours.
PLINY THE ELDER *Natural History* VII 20

A journey from Rome to the River Rhône, France

Julius Caesar got most of his sleep while he travelled in chariots or in litters (sedan-chairs carried by slaves). He travelled very fast. For example on his first journey from Rome, he reached the River Rhône in Southern France (a distance of approximately 650 miles from Rome) in 7 days.
PLUTARCH *Life of Caesar* 17 5

A journey in Egypt

The journey from Coptus (in Egypt) to the town of Berenice on the Red Sea 257 miles away is made on camel, and there are staging-posts at intervals for watering. . . . Most of the journey is covered at night because of the heat during the day, and the days are spent at staging-posts. The whole journey from Coptus to Berenice takes 12 days.
PLINY THE ELDER *Natural History* VI 26

Camel transport in Tunisia

Finding your way

If he wanted to find out the route through a country or which road to take, the Roman traveller would ask the way whenever he came to a new town or enquire from other road users, like traders, who knew the road. He could also look up travellers' guides and road maps.

Travellers' guides or 'itineraries' (from the Latin word **itinera** = journeys) were published, listing the roads throughout the Roman Empire and the names of the towns and staging-posts along them with the distances between each. The most famous of these is the so-called **Antonine Itinerary** which was probably published about 280 AD. The extract shown here is one of the Roman routes in Britain, the road from London to Dover.

Note: ITER = Total distance in Roman miles

M.P. = *milia passuum* or 'miles'

Extract from the Antonine Itinerary covering Roman roads in Britain. This part shows Route III: London to Dover.

	Roman miles	English miles	
Iter a Londinio ad portum Dubris m.p. sic.	LXVI	$68\frac{3}{4}$	From London to Dover Port
Durobrivis	XXVII	$28\frac{3}{4}$	Rochester
Duroverno	XXV	$25\frac{1}{2}$	Canterbury
Ad portum Dubris	XIIII	$14\frac{1}{2}$	Dover Port

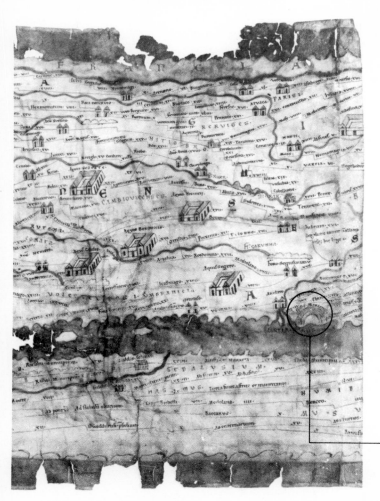

The Romans also used road maps, which were copies of a large map carved in marble which stood in the Forum at Rome showing the main roads throughout the Empire. In the fifteenth century a copy (probably made in the third century AD) was found and given to a man named Conrad Peutinger who lived at Augsburg in Germany. The map, which is on parchment, does not look much like a modern map. It is more like a diagram showing the London Underground system. Instead of worrying about accuracy of scale and direction, the Romans drew it to show the main road routes, towns and staging-posts with the distances between each marked in with Roman numbers.

The extract shown here is part of the **Peutinger Table** showing Marseilles (called Ostia Rhodani by the Romans) at the mouth of the River Rhône (Rhodanus). The land at the top of the map is Europe and at the very top you can see the word FRANCIA, the Mediaeval name for modern France. The narrow strip at the bottom is North Africa (you can see the name Numid(arum), the Roman name for modern Libya, in capital letters if you look carefully.) The grey strip between the two is the Mediterranean Sea.

Compare this with a modern map of this part of the Mediterranean in your atlas.

Marseilles

Part of the Peutinger Table showing Marseilles (Ostia Rhodani) in the South of France

QUESTIONS

1 How many different forms of transport did Horace use on his journey from Rome to Brundisium? (pages 22–23) What was the average distance he travelled in a day?

2 What kind of transport would be used by
   a) poor people and peasants?
   b) rich people and government officials?

3 What three problems of road travel are mentioned in the extracts on page 25?

4 Who started the Imperial Post? What was it? How do we know? (page 26)

5 Why were there staging-posts for official couriers? Where did ordinary Roman travellers spend the night? (page 27)

6 Work out the average distances covered per day by the travellers mentioned on pages 22 and 28. Make a table listing the route, method of travel, distance travelled and average mileage per day. Calculate average speed per hour if you can. How fast did an official messenger travel? (page 27)

7 What information could a traveller get from an itinerary like the one on page 29 and the road map on page 30? Give examples from each. How else could a traveller get information about which route to take?

THINGS TO DO

1 Make a wall-chart comparing Roman and modern types of road transport.

2 Imagine you are *either* an official courier with an important message *or* an ordinary traveller. Write a story describing your journey, including where you are going, how you travel, where you spend the night, and any adventures you have on the way.

3 Imagine you are *either* an angry customer complaining to an inn-keeper about your stay at his inn, *or* a traveller who has seen the advertisement for a room with three beds shown on page 27. Write a dialogue between yourself and the inn-keeper.

4 Compare the section of the Peutinger Table on page 30 with a modern AA sectional route map. In what ways are they similar and in what ways different?

4: ROME: MARKET-PLACE OF THE WORLD

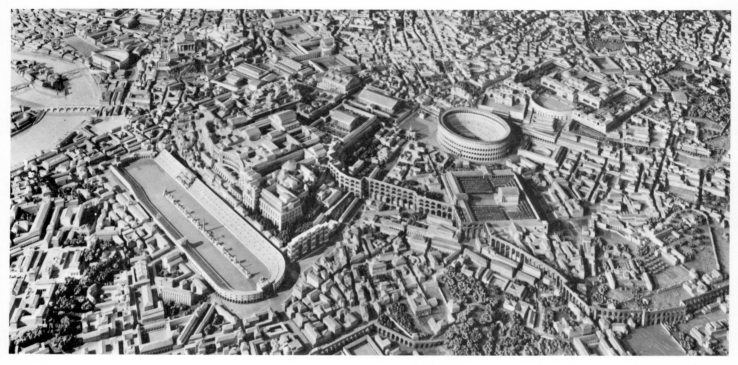

A model showing what Rome looked like about 300 AD.
Can you recognise any of the buildings?

Capital of an Empire

By the end of the first century AD Rome was the capital of an empire made up of forty-three provinces. The city had grown from a small settlement founded by Romulus in 753 BC beside the River Tiber into a large centre of government and trade with a population probably of about one million inhabitants (about the same population as Glasgow, Manchester or Birmingham). It was a sprawling mass of tenements, shops and market-places (**emporia**), to which travellers from all parts of the Roman world came for trading or on official business.

Rome served as a market-place for the countries round the Mediterranean Sea. One writer in the second century AD remarked:

Around the Mediterranean Sea (which the Romans called the *Mare Clausum* or 'Closed Sea') lie the continents (of Europe, Asia, and Africa) . . . pouring an endless flow of goods into Rome. To Rome is transported by land and sea whatever is produced. . . . What you cannot see here does not exist.

AELIUS ARISTIDES *To Rome* XI–XIII

What kind of things would a large city like Rome have needed to import from other countries in order to support a population of about one million people?

The Forum in Rome, showing the Capitoline Hill

Roman Empire in the 1st century AD showing the main goods and products supplied by the provinces

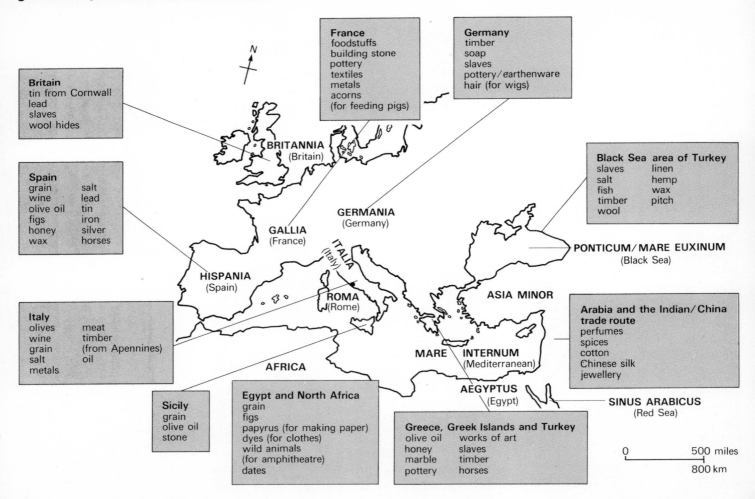

Britain
tin from Cornwall
lead
slaves
wool hides

Spain
grain   salt
wine   lead
olive oil   tin
figs   iron
honey   silver
wax   horses

Italy
olives   meat
wine   timber
grain   (from Apennines)
salt   oil
metals

France
foodstuffs
building stone
pottery
textiles
metals
acorns
(for feeding pigs)

Germany
timber
soap
slaves
pottery/earthenware
hair (for wigs)

Black Sea area of Turkey
slaves   linen
salt   hemp
fish   wax
timber   pitch
wool

Arabia and the Indian/China trade route
perfumes
spices
cotton
Chinese silk
jewellery

Sicily
grain
olive oil
stone

Egypt and North Africa
grain
figs
papyrus (for making paper)
dyes (for clothes)
wild animals
(for amphitheatre)
dates

Greece, Greek Islands and Turkey
olive oil   works of art
honey   slaves
marble   timber
pottery   horses

N

BRITANNIA
(Britain)

GERMANIA
(Germany)

GALLIA
(France)

HISPANIA
(Spain)

ITALIA
(Italy)

ROMA
(Rome)

AFRICA

ASIA MINOR

MARE   INTERNUM
(Mediterranean)

AEGYPTUS
(Egypt)

PONTICUM/MARE EUXINUM
(Black Sea)

SINUS ARABICUS
(Red Sea)

0   500 miles
800 km

The grain supply

The most important of all the goods imported into Rome was grain to make bread. Many of Rome's one million inhabitants were poor or unemployed citizens on the dole who were entitled to free bread each day. If there was a bad grain harvest in Egypt or Sicily, there was a shortage of bread, which led to riots in the streets as hungry people angrily demanded food and fought for what they could get.

In 42 AD after bread riots in the previous years due to the shortage of grain, the Emperor Claudius ordered a new harbour to be built at the mouth of the River Tiber at Portus. (Until this the main port of Rome had been Puteoli, modern Pozzuoli, near Naples.) This harbour was designed to take grain ships with cargoes of 65 tons (10,000 **modii*** or 'measures') and over, and Claudius offered Roman citizenship to owners who built ships that could carry such quantities of grain and shipped it for at least six years.

An enormous amount of grain was needed to feed Rome's population of one million. In fact we are told by one Roman writer that during the reign of Augustus (27 BC–14 AD) the Romans imported 150,000 tons (or 20,000,000 measures) of grain from Egypt each year. In order to handle such large quantities of foodstuffs and all the other goods from the provinces, they needed good harbour and warehouse facilities.

Dealers measuring corn shown on a mosaic from the Square of the Shipping Corporations in Ostia (see page 37)

* I modius = 1·92 gallons

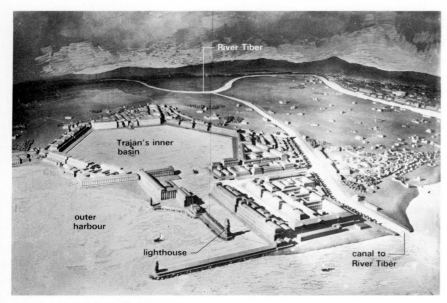

River Tiber

Trajan's inner basin

outer harbour

lighthouse

canal to River Tiber

Model of the Claudian harbour at Portus showing the outer harbour and Trajan's inner basin. In the background you can see the River Tiber.

Portus—gateway to Rome

In 114 AD, just over seventy years later, the Emperor Trajan enlarged the outer harbour built by Claudius and also built an inner basin to provide a completely sheltered anchorage for up to 200 ships.

The harbour at Portus had all the facilities needed for the international import and export of goods. There was a lighthouse marking the entrance between the two break-waters of the outer harbour. Round the two basins were facilities for building and repairing ships, cranes for loading and unloading cargoes, warehouses for storing goods awaiting shipment, and the premises of all the different people involved in shipping—shipwrights, sailmakers, ropemakers, dockers, and so on.

Large sea-going ships were too big to sail up the River Tiber to Rome itself. So most of the cargoes arriving from abroad were unloaded at Portus and then loaded into smaller river boats that could sail up the River Tiber. The inner basin built by Trajan was linked directly to the Tiber by a canal for this purpose, as you can see in the model on this page.

Ostia—commercial centre for the shipping trade

In the nearby town of Ostia were the offices and warehouses of the shipping companies (called **navicularii** from the Latin word **navis** = ship).

Each of the different shipping companies had its own offices at Ostia as we can see from the mosaics that have been found in the so-called Square of the Shipping Corporations, like the one shown on page 35. There were also money-lenders to put up the money for business ventures.

Ostia was a commercial centre where fortunes were made and lost in contracts for transporting cargoes such as grain, wine and olive oil from the provinces around the Mediterranean to Italy.

The shipping trade could be very profitable but was also a risky business. Disasters were quite common, as we can see from the wrecks of ships that have been discovered by marine archaeologists and accounts like the following.

Trimalchio's business ventures

I decided to go into the shipping business. I had five ships built and loaded them with wine, which was fetching a high price at that time, and shipped them off to Rome. What a disaster! All five were wrecked. In one day the old sea-god Neptune swallowed down a million's worth of wine. But I wasn't beat, not me! I built some more—bigger, better ones and luckier. I shipped a cargo of wine, bacon, beans, perfumes and slaves.
PETRONIUS *Satyricon* 76

A merchant paying tax for the transporting of goods. Notice the tax-collector counting the money on the table.

A man measuring grain

Taxes, weights and measures

At the main ports and border posts throughout the Roman Empire there were customs officers or tax collectors (called **conductores**) whose job was to collect the taxes charged on all imports and exports that passed through. There were also weights and measures inspectors who checked that the right quantities of goods were loaded and unloaded, and that cargoes had not been tampered with or damaged during the journey.

Grain was measured in **modii**, or 'measures', and handled in sacks of a size one man could carry. Olive oil and wine were shipped in jars (**amphorae**) made of clay which held 20–30 litres each; each jar plus contents probably weighed about 50 kilogrammes. So a cargo of 10,000 jars weighed about 500 tons, while 60,000 'measures' of grain weighed 400 tons. (These figures are only approximate because we cannot be sure.)

Here is part of the regulations used by customs officers to work out how much tax to charge, and some of the rules about what should happen if someone was found to be trying to smuggle goods through by not declaring them.

Except for methods of transport (for example, boats) all articles shall be subject to a tax of $2\frac{1}{2}$% (of their value), payable to the tax collector. The tax collector has the right of search. Any articles that have not been declared shall be confiscated. A married woman, however, may not be searched.

PSEUDO-QUINTILIAN *Declamations* CCCLIX

QUESTIONS

1 What did the Romans call the Mediterranean Sea? Why was it so important to them? (page 33)
2 Why does the writer of the description on page 33 say 'What you cannot see here does not exist'?
3 Who built the harbour at Portus? When? Why was it built? (page 35)
4 Why did Claudius offer Roman citizenship to certain ship-owners? On what conditions? (page 35)
5 Look at the map on page 34 and write down the countries from which the Romans imported the following: grain, oil, salt, wool, cotton, wax, spices, metals (like tin and silver), pottery, and slaves. What would each have been used for?
6 Who organised Roman shipping trade? Where did they get the money for their business from? (page 37)
7 How had Trimalchio lost a fortune? (page 37) What did he do after this?
8 What are the men in the photograph at the bottom of page 37 doing?
9 Why were there customs officers at Roman ports? What rate of tax did they charge traders? What happened if someone did not declare some of the cargo? (page 38) How do we know?

THINGS TO DO

1 Make a list of the things a Roman family would need for everyday living—for example, food, clothing, heating, etc. Then list the countries from which each of these came using the map on page 34.
2 You are a Roman ship-owner. Make a list of all the other people and facilities you need to carry on your business—for example, ship-builders and repairers, harbour facilities, and so on.
3 Write an imaginary dialogue between a Roman customs officer trying to enforce the rules on page 38 and the captain of a ship trying to smuggle something past him.

5: SHIPS AND SEA-FARING

The tombstone of a boat-builder called Publius Longidienus, showing his son building a coaster using the 'shell-first' method.

Roman ships were of two main types—small coastal or river boats, and larger sea-going cargo ships. There were also smaller craft like tug-boats, canal boats and ferries used on inland waterways.

Coastal and river boats

Small coasters, like the Isis Giminiana in the photograph on page 6, were used for carrying cargoes along the coast and up rivers too small for larger ships to navigate. They were called **naves caudicariae** (or 'ships with tails', because of their high curved prows and sterns).

These coasters could carry cargoes of up to 70–80 tons (*either* 10,000 measures of grain *or* 1,000 jars of wine or oil) after they had been unloaded from larger sea-going freighters. They were built using the 'shell-first' method. The hull, or shell, of the boat was built first with planks, and then strengthened with frames inside. The photograph here shows a boat-builder using an adze to shape one of these frames. The hull of the boat lies already completed on the stocks.

A sea-going freighter passing a lighthouse as it leaves port

Sea-going freighters

Sea-going freighters called **naves onerariae** (or 'cargo-carrying ships') varied in size and in the amount of cargo they could carry. Below is a table showing the specifications for an average-sized freighter.

Larger cargo ships like the one in the photograph were referred to as '10,000ers' — i.e. they could carry up to 10,000 jars or 60,000 measures of grain (about 350–500 tons of cargo).

Specifications of an average-sized Roman cargo ship

Length (overall):	75–90 feet (25–30 metres)
Width (or beam):	24–30 feet (8–10 metres)
Cargo capacity:	110–180 tons of cargo
either:	30,000 'measures' of grain
or:	3,000 jars of wine or oil
Total weight when loaded:	250–350 tons
Steering:	2 steering oars, 1 on each side at the stern
Propulsion:	1 mainsail (square-rigged) 1 foresail (called an *artemon*) Oars for use in port
Average speed (with a favourable wind behind):	4–6 knots per hour 70–90 sea miles per day

The photograph here of a marble relief shows a cargo ship entering Portus with a lighthouse in the background. Notice the deckhouse, the cabins, the curved swan's head at the stern, the large steering oar and the large main sail with two pictures of Romulus and Remus being suckled by the she-wolf, as in the legend of the founding of Rome.

If you look carefully you can see the ship's master and passengers standing on deck at the stern (on the left) in front of a fire. They are offering a sacrifice of thanksgiving to the gods for their safe arrival.

Bulk grain carriers

The Romans also built some super-freighters for carrying large cargoes of grain from Alexandria (in Egypt) to Portus or Puteoli. These bulk carriers could carry up to 100,000 measures of grain (680 tons) or 15,000 jars (750 tons) on one voyage, and had a total weight when laden of about 1250 tons. The drawing on this page shows one of these grain ships called the Europa.

The writer Lucian described another of these super-freighters called the 'Isis' (after the Egyptian goddess Isis). Below is a table comparing the size of the 'Isis', based on Lucian's description, with the size of a modern bulk carrier.

Drawing found in Pompeii of a grain ship called the 'Europa'

The 'Isis'

Length:	180 feet (55 metres)
Width of beam:	45 feet (14 metres)
Height (from deck to keel):	44 feet (13 metres)
Overall tonnage when loaded:	about 1,250 tons

Modern bulk carrier (for grain)

Length:	750 feet (229 metres)
Width of beam:	100 feet (30 metres)
Height (from deck to keel):	65 feet (20 metres)
Overall tonnage when loaded:	65,000 tons

44

The journey of the Isis

Lucian describes a voyage made by the 'Isis' on one of its runs from Egypt to Italy. Below is part of his description.

They set sail from the **pharos** (or lighthouse) at Alexandria with a moderate wind, and on the seventh day sighted Cape Acamas (at the northern tip of Cyprus). Then a west wind blew up and carried them off course to Sidon (modern Saida, just south of Beirut in Lebanon).

After leaving Sidon they were caught in a heavy gale, and on the tenth day passed through the straits at Cape Gelidonia (the southern tip of Turkey between Rhodes and Cyprus). They nearly went to the bottom there on a pitch black night.

But the gods heard their cries and showed them a beacon, and a bright star, either Castor or Pollux, appeared at the masthead and guided them into open sea on the port (left) side just as they were heading straight for cliffs.

Then after straying off course they sailed through the Aegean Sea, beating up against adverse north-easterly winds, until they came to anchor yesterday in Piraeus (the port of Athens), seventy days after leaving Egypt because they had been blown so far off course. If they had sailed their normal course, they should have passed Crete on the starboard (right) side, rounded Cape Malea (the southern tip of Greece), and been in Italy by this time.

LUCIAN *The Ship* 5–9

Two cargo ships passing a lighthouse.
Notice the beacon on top of the lighthouse.

Table of Average Sailing Times*

Journey	Length (miles)	Overall time (days)	Overall speed (knots)
Portus – N. Africa	270	2	6
Portus – Gibraltar	935	7	5·6
Puteoli – Alexandria	1,000	9	4·6
Messina – Alexandria	830	7	5

* made with favourable winds

Navigation techniques and sailing seasons

The Romans were not really a seafaring-race. They had to learn the art of ship-building and navigation (from the Greeks and other nations with whom they traded).

Sailors in the ancient world had no compass, sextant or navigation charts by which to plot their course accurately. The only maps available were very vague and, although by the first century AD it had been proved that the earth was round, people thought the world was a flat disc and that if you sailed far enough you would fall off the edge.

Roman sailors, like the Greeks, usually sailed close to land, putting into port at night if they could. To plot a course they followed the coast where possible, looking for well-known landmarks, and used their knowledge of the sun and the winds that blew in different directions at different times of the year. On long journeys across open sea at night they steered by the stars. On dangerous coasts there were sometimes beacons to warn sailors of cliffs and rocks. But if you were caught in a storm the only thing to do was to lower the sails and run before the wind.

The sailing season lasted only about four months.

From the 27th of May until the 14th of September is thought to be the safe period for sailing. . . . From then till the 10th of November is doubtful. . . . And from the 10th of November until the 10th of March the seas are closed.
VEGETIUS *On Military Matters* IV 39

The only sailing that went on during the winter and early spring was by ships carrying urgent supplies and messages. Some ship-owners and captains sometimes took a risk and tried to sail during the winter, with disastrous results as you can see from the description on the next page.

Shipwrecked

On his journey to Rome as a prisoner, the grain ship on which Paul and the others were sailing reached Crete at the end of the safe season for sailing. In spite of advice to wait until the spring, the captain decided to go on. Below is part of Paul's account of what happened.

We were sailing along the coast of Crete when a storm called the 'North-easter' struck us and we had to give way and run before it. After running under the lee of a small island, the crew braced the ship's hull with ropes and chains, and then lowered the sails and ran before the storm. . . . Because they were being tossed about violently, next day they began to throw the cargo overboard, and on the third day threw overboard the ship's tackle. After we had seen neither sun nor stars for many days, and the storm was still raging, we gave up all hope of being saved. . . .

On the fourteenth night at about midnight the sailors suspected we were nearing land. So they took soundings (with a lead weight at the end of a line) and found that the depth was 20 fathoms.* Afraid of running onto rocks, they threw out four sea-anchors from the stern and prayed for daylight. Next morning when the seventy-six people on board had eaten, they threw the corn overboard to lighten the ship. At dawn they saw land which they did not recognise. After casting off the anchors and loosening the ropes that held the steering oars, they hoisted sail and ran towards the beach. But the ship struck a shoal and ran aground. The bow stuck and the stern began to break up in the surf. Then the centurion ordered those who could to swim ashore. The rest escaped by using planks and pieces of the ship.

Acts of the Apostles 27 (adapted)

* 1 fathom = 6 feet.

The Roman lighthouse at Dover today

QUESTIONS

1 What kind of ships were:
   a) the 'Isis Giminiana' (pages 6 and 40)?
   b) the 'Isis' and the 'Europa' (page 43)?
   How much cargo could each carry? How do we know
   their names and what they were like?
2 What kind of ship is shown in the photograph on page
   42? How do we know that it is entering harbour at the
   end of a voyage?
3 How long had the 'Isis' taken to sail from Alexandria
   to Athens? Why? What was the normal time taken by
   a ship sailing direct from Alexandria to Puteoli near
   Naples? (pages 44 and 45)
4 How did Roman sailors navigate during the day and at
   night? What had helped the crew of the 'Isis' to avoid
   being wrecked on cliffs? (pages 44 and 45)
5 What was the normal sailing season? How do we
   know? And why did some ships sail during the
   'closed' season? (page 45)
6 What kind of ship were Paul and the others travelling
   on? (pages 6 and 46) What advice had the captain
   ignored? How do we know what happened?
7 What did the crew do when the storm struck? How
   did they try to save the ship during the next two days?
   (page 46) Why could they not plot a course?
8 How did the crew tell they were near land? How did
   they try to save the ship? What happened? (page 46)
9 How many people were on board? How did they
   manage to escape? (page 46)

THINGS TO DO

1 Make a wall-chart comparing Roman and modern
   cargo ships. Alongside each picture write a short
   description including size, type and quantity of cargo
   carried, its name, and typical route(s) sailed.
2 Imagine you are the master of a Roman grain ship
   bound for Italy. *Either* explain to an angry ship-owner
   why you have arrived later than you ought
   Or write a story describing how you were saved from
   being shipwrecked in a storm.

SOME IMPORTANT DATES

BC	**753**	Foundation of Rome by Romulus
	312	First recorded paved road built by Appius Claudius from Rome to Capua
	241	Via Aurelia built from Rome to Pisa
	220	Via Flaminia built from Rome to Ariminum
	187	Via Aemilia built from Ariminum to Placentia
	177	Via Cassia built from Rome to Aretium
	149–6	Via Postumia built from Genoa to Cremona
	148–32	Via Flaminia extended from Ariminum to Brundisium
	145	Via Egnatia built from Jugoslavia to Greece
	140–25	Via Cassia extended from Arretium to Pisa
	132	Via Popilia built from Capua to Rhegium
	123	First Roman milestones erected alongside roads
	120	Roman road built over the Alps
	38	The Roman poet Horace travelled from Rome to Brundisium
AD	**8**	Emperor Augustus started the Imperial Postal Service
		The Pont du Gard aqueduct built near Nîmes, France
	42	Harbour at Portus near Ostia built by Emperor Claudius
		Via Ostiensis rebuilt by Emperor Claudius
	43	Roman invasion and beginning of road network in Britain
	74–81	Road network in Britain extended during Agricola's campaigns
	80	Via Domitiana built from Sinuessa to Naples
	93–113	Via Nerva-Traiana built from Carthage to Alexandria in N. Africa
	105	Bridge across the R. Tagus in Spain built by G. Julius Lacer
	109	Via Aemilia Scauri extended the Via Aurelia; Milvian Bridge at Rome built
	114	Emperor Trajan extended the harbour at Portus
	c280	Antonine Itinerary of routes throughout the Empire published
	c410	Roman legions withdrawn from Britain